# TEAM SPIRIT ®

## SMART BOOKS FOR YOUNG FANS

# THE OKLAHOMA CITY THUNDER

BY

MARK STEWART

NORWOOD HOUSE PRESS

CHICAGO, ILLINOIS

Norwood House Press
P.O. Box 316598
Chicago, Illinois 60631

For information regarding Norwood House Press, please visit our website at:
www.norwoodhousepress.com or call 866-565-2900.

All photos courtesy of Associated Press except the following:
Pacific Northwest Bell (6), Seattle Supersonics (7, 16, 33, 34 left, 42 top), Beckett Publications (10, 35 top left),
Topps, Inc. (7, 15, 17, 22, 30, 35 top right, 38, 42 bottom, 45), The Sporting News (19), The Star Company (21),
Panini America, Inc. (23), Author's Collection (28), Dexter Press (31), Editions Rencontre (34 right),
SportsChrome (35 bottom, 42 bottom, 43 top), JBC/NBA Hoops (40).
Cover Photo: Sue Ogrocki/Associated Press

The memorabilia and artifacts pictured in this book are presented for educational and informational purposes,
and come from the collection of the author.

Editor: Mike Kennedy
Designer: Ron Jaffe
Project Management: Black Book Partners, LLC.
Special thanks to Topps, Inc.

Library of Congress Cataloging-in-Publication Data

Stewart, Mark, 1960 July 7-
  The Oklahoma City Thunder / by Mark Stewart.
     pages cm. -- (Team spirit)
  Includes bibliographical references and index.
  Summary: "A revised Team Spirit Basketball edition featuring the Oklahoma
City Thunder that chronicles the history and accomplishments of the team.
Includes access to the Team Spirit website which provides additional
information and photos"-- Provided by publisher.
  ISBN 978-1-59953-639-2 (library edition : alk. paper) -- ISBN
978-1-60357-648-2 (ebook)
  1.  Oklahoma City Thunder (Basketball team)--History--Juvenile literature.
2.  Basketball--Oklahoma--Oklahoma City--History--Juvenile literature.  I.
Title.
  GV885.52.O37S74 2014
  796.323'640976638--dc23

                                            2014007735

253N—072014
Manufactured in the United States of America in North Mankato, Minnesota.

**COVER PHOTO**: The Thunder get their fans excited by working hard on both
ends of the court.

# Table of Contents

**ABOUT OUR GLOSSARY**

In this book, there may be several words that you are reading for the first time. Some are sports words, some are new vocabulary words, and some are familiar words that are used in an unusual way. All of these words are defined on page 46. Throughout the book, sports words appear in **bold type**. Regular vocabulary words appear in *bold italic type*.

# Meet the Thunder

**C**an **professional** basketball make it in Oklahoma? That was the question on people's minds in 2008 when the Seattle Supersonics moved to the state and were renamed the Oklahoma City Thunder. The answer came in just a few games. The players were welcomed like old friends. Not even a slow start could dim the fans' enthusiasm.

The Thunder won over their fans the same way they win division titles. They find exciting stars and smart, unselfish players to support them. They hire coaches who encourage team spirit. And they rely on their fans for an extra boost of energy whenever they need it.

This book tells the story of the Thunder. Much of it takes place in the *Pacific Northwest*, where the team played for more than 40 years and won a championship. The Thunder have their sights set on building on that success.

Kevin Durant and Serge Ibaka are fired up after a good play during a 2013–14 game. Oklahoma has proven to be a great home for the Thunder.

# Glory Days

The story of the Thunder began 2,000 miles from Oklahoma City, in Seattle, Washington. The Supersonics—or "Sonics" for short—joined the **National Basketball Association (NBA)** in 1967 when the league expanded from 10 to 12 teams. Seattle's first victory came over the San Diego Rockets, the NBA's other new team that year. The Rockets now play in Houston.

The Sonics faced the challenge of building their team from  unwanted and unproven players. This was even more difficult because a new league formed in 1967, the **American Basketball Association (ABA)**. The ABA competed for many of the same players.

During the first few seasons in Seattle, the team starred Lenny Wilkens, Bob Rule, and Tom Meschery. Wilkens became **player-coach** of the Sonics in 1969–70. That same season, he led the NBA in **assists** and was named an **All-Star**!

Competition between the NBA and ABA in the early 1970s drove up salaries in pro basketball. Seattle's owner, Sam Schulman, thought the best solution was to *merge* the leagues. To get the attention of NBA owners, he threatened to move the Sonics to California and join the ABA. Eventually, the NBA agreed with Schulman, the Sonics stayed put, and the leagues joined forces for the 1976–77 season.

In the meantime, Schulman made headlines by signing the ABA's top

OFFICIAL 1972-73 PRESS, RADIO, TELEVISION GUIDE

$1.00

player, Spencer Haywood. In 1971–72, Haywood led the Sonics to their first winning season. Two years later, another big name came to Seattle when **Hall of Famer** Bill Russell was signed to coach the club. Russell had won 11 championships with the Boston Celtics. He guided Seattle to a second-place finish in the **Pacific Division**. The Sonics had two exciting guards during this *era*, "Downtown" Fred Brown and Donald "Slick" Watts. Brown was famous for his long-distance shooting. Watts specialized in defense.

**LEFT**: This postcard shows Seattle's first winning team.
**ABOVE**: As this old guide shows, high-flying Spencer Haywood was the star of the Sonics in the 1970s.

In 1977–78, the Sonics put together one of the best young teams in the NBA. They brought Wilkens back to coach the club. Gus Williams and Dennis Johnson were his starting guards, and Jack Sikma and Marvin Webster shared time at center. With help from **veterans** such as Brown, John Johnson, and Paul Silas, the Sonics reached the **NBA Finals** and came within one victory of defeating the Washington Bullets for the championship.

They finished the job the following year. The Sonics lost Webster as a **free agent**, but they added forward Lonnie Shelton. Seattle faced a rematch in the 1979 NBA Finals with Washington. This time, the Sonics could not be stopped and won their first championship.

New stars led the Sonics in the 1980s, including Dale Ellis, Tom Chambers, Nate McMillan, Derrick McKey, and Xavier McDaniel. Seattle made it to the finals of the **Western Conference** in 1986–87, but the team lost to the powerhouse Los Angeles Lakers. Not until the 1990s did the Sonics reach the NBA Finals again. That team, coached by George Karl, featured two of the NBA's most dynamic players, Shawn Kemp and Gary Payton.

**LEFT**: Gus Williams floats to the rim for a layup against the Bullets in the NBA Finals. **ABOVE**: Tom Chambers averaged 20 points a game in five seasons in Seattle.

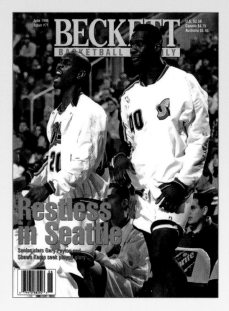

Kemp was an amazing athlete who specialized in power dunks. Many of those came on **alley-oop** passes from Payton, who was a top scorer, playmaker, and defender. This duo teamed with Sam Perkins, Hersey Hawkins, Ervin Johnson, and Detlef Schrempf to survive a seven-game war with the Utah Jazz in the 1996 **Western Conference Finals**. Unfortunately, Seattle's third trip to the NBA Finals ended in a loss to the Chicago Bulls. The Sonics had plenty of talent, but they lacked the confidence to defeat Michael Jordan and his teammates.

In six seasons under Karl, the Sonics became one of the NBA's best teams, but they never delivered a championship. After Karl left the club, Seattle made the **playoffs** just three times in 10 seasons. The team had plenty of good players, including Ray Allen, Rashard Lewis, and Luke Ridnour. However, it didn't have a superstar who could put the Sonics over the top and fill the seats in their arena.

In 2007, Seattle took Kevin Durant in the NBA **draft**. Durant was just 19 years old, but he already showed the talent and leadership to turn the Sonics into a championship **contender**. Team owner Clay Bennett hoped to give Durant and his teammates a new arena in Seattle. But he did not see eye-to-eye with the city. Bennett decided to move the club to Oklahoma City for the 2008–09 season. After a horrible 3–29 start, the newly renamed Thunder regrouped and finished the year with 20 wins in their final 50 games.

The following year, the Thunder improved to 50 victories, and Durant won the first of three NBA scoring titles. Two young guards—Russell Westbrook and James Harden—had great seasons. Danny Green, Thabo Sefolosha, and Serge Ibaka also contributed to the team's success. In 2010–11, the Thunder added center Kendrick Perkins. They won 55 games and advanced to the Western Conference Finals.

The team made it all the way to the NBA Finals in 2011–12. It took the powerful Miami Heat to beat the Thunder in a championship showdown. Oklahoma City fans had come close to their first championship and would never forget the joy and excitement their team had brought them.

**LEFT**: Gary Payton and Shawn Kemp gave "restless" Sonics fans something to cheer for in the 1990s.  **ABOVE**: Kevin Durant helped make the Thunder a championship contender.

The Thunder play in an arena located in downtown Oklahoma City. It was built in 2002 and served as the home of the New Orleans Hornets (now Pelicans) after Hurricane Katrina in 2005. The people of Oklahoma City approved a plan to upgrade the arena. It will be one of the most modern facilities in the NBA.

During its days as the Sonics, the team had three homes, including the Seattle Center Coliseum and Tacoma Dome. Their most famous home was the Kingdome. It was one of the NBA's noisiest arenas, and the team set many attendance records there.

## BY THE NUMBERS

- The Thunder's arena has 18,203 seats for basketball.
- The court sits 22 feet below street level.
- As of 2013–14, the Thunder (and Sonics) had retired six uniform numbers—1 (Gus Williams), 10 (Nate McMillan), 19 (Lenny Wilkens), 24 (Spencer Haywood), 32 (Fred Brown), and 43 (Jack Sikma).

Russell Westbrook rises for a dunk on the Thunder's home court.

# Dressed for Success

Oklahoma City's colors are orange-red, white, and two shades of blue. Orange-red honors Oklahoma State University and the University of Oklahoma. Their football teams are the most popular in the state. The Thunder's **logo** shows a shield with *OKC*, which is short for "Oklahoma City."

When the Sonics played in Seattle, their colors were green, gold, and white. The team used the shortened version of its name—*Sonics*—on its uniforms. During the 1990s, Seattle added red as a uniform color for a few years. The name "Supersonics" recognized the businesses in the Pacific Northwest that helped build military jets. Supersonic means faster than the speed of sound.

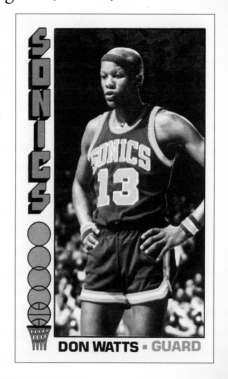

DON WATTS ▪ GUARD

**LEFT**: Reggie Jackson scans the defense during a 2013–14 road game.
**ABOVE**: Slick Watts wears the green Seattle uniform of the 1970s.

# We Won!

The Sonics won the NBA championship once while they played in Seattle. The title came in the spring of 1979, the team's 12th season. The year before, the Sonics advanced to the NBA Finals for the first time. They faced off against the Washington Bullets, and came within a game of the championship. The Bullets had a great team with an awesome front line of Elvin Hayes, Wes Unseld, and Bob Dandridge. After Seattle's loss in Game 7, Sonics fans were understandably disappointed. But forward Paul Silas looked on the bright side. He felt that coming so close to the NBA title and then losing to the experienced Bullets would help the young team in the future. Silas was right.

The Sonics improved by five victories during the 1978–79 season. In the playoffs, they beat the Los Angeles Lakers, and then survived a tough seven-game series with the Phoenix Suns in the Western Conference Finals. That set up a rematch with the Bullets in the NBA Finals.

The Sonics had great depth at every position. Their three guards—Gus Williams, Dennis Johnson, and Fred Brown—were brilliant at both ends of the court. The team's front line included Silas and forwards

**FRED BROWN · G**

John Johnson and Lonnie Shelton. When center Jack Sikma needed a break, Shelton moved over to take his place. Coach Lenny Wilkens knew how to get the most out of everyone on the roster.

The Bullets were confident they could defend their championship. This was their fourth trip to the NBA Finals during the 1970s, and they had the NBA's best record in 1978–79. Seattle's

**LEFT**: Paul Silas was an important leader for the 1978–79 Sonics.
**ABOVE**: Fred Brown was the team's most dangerous outside shooter.

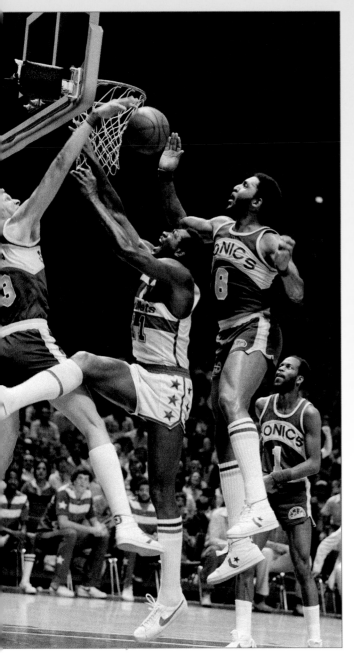

advantage was that the Bullets needed seven games to defeat the Atlanta Hawks and San Antonio Spurs to reach the finals. Wilkens believed the older Washington players might be wearing down. Although the Bullets won Game 1, it took a big night from backup guard Larry Wright to do so.

Game 2 was a different story, even though the Bullets built another early lead. This time, the Sonics dug in on defense and made an impressive comeback. They held the Bullets to just 30 points in the second half and won going away, 92–82. The Seattle guards were the stars of the game.

Williams, Johnson, and Brown were even better in Game 3. They bombed away for 64 points. The Sonics took the series lead with a 105–95 victory.

Game 4 was a thrilling contest. After four quarters, the score was tied, 104–104. Sikma was sensational for the Sonics. In the final moments of the fourth period, he swatted away three shots to help send the contest into **overtime**. Seattle outscored the Bullets in the extra period for a 114–112 victory.

In Game 5, Hayes nearly buried the Sonics by himself. He scored 20 points in the first half. However, Washington's starting guards both suffered injuries, and this time their backups did not get the job done. Seattle's backcourt stars took over and led a comeback. Williams scored 23 points—the fifth game in a row he topped the team in scoring. The Sonics held on for a 97–93 victory to give Seattle its first NBA championship.

Voting for the **Most Valuable Player (MVP)** was tough. Williams and Sikma both deserved consideration, but the trophy went to Dennis Johnson. He averaged 22 points and six assists per game. "DJ" also played great defense.

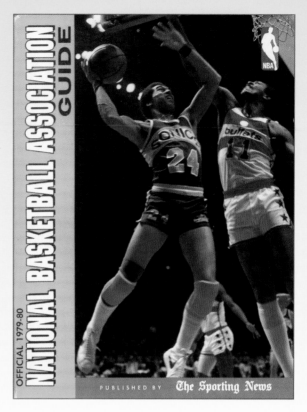

**LEFT**: Jack Sikma and Lonnie Shelton put the clamps on Elvin Hayes during the 1979 NBA Finals. **ABOVE**: Dennis Johnson was named MVP of the series for the Sonics. He appeared on the NBA's annual guide the following season.

To be a true star in the NBA, you need more than a great shot. You have to be a "go-to guy"—someone teammates trust to make the winning play when the seconds are ticking away in a big game. Sonics and Thunder fans have had a lot to cheer about over the years, including these great stars …

## THE PIONEERS

### LENNY WILKENS                                    6′ 1″ Guard

• BORN: 10/28/1937    • PLAYED FOR TEAM: 1968–69 TO 1971–72

Lenny Wilkens gave the Sonics an experienced leader in their early years. He led the NBA in assists twice. In both of those seasons, he was also Seattle's player-coach!

### SPENCER HAYWOOD                                 6′ 9″ Forward

• BORN: 4/22/1949    • PLAYED FOR TEAM: 1970–71 TO 1974–75

Spencer Haywood was the top prize in the battle between the NBA and ABA. He joined the Sonics after a long legal fight. In Haywood's third year with the team, he averaged 29 points and nearly 13 rebounds a game. Kevin Durant broke his scoring record, but Haywood's rebounding mark still stands.

## FRED BROWN                                    6´ 3˝ Guard

- BORN: 8/7/1948    • PLAYED FOR TEAM:  1971–72 TO 1983–84

Fred Brown was known as "Downtown," because he liked to launch shots far from the basket. Brown played every minute of his career in Seattle. Though he rarely started, he averaged nearly 15 points a game.

## DENNIS JOHNSON                                6´ 4˝ Guard

- BORN: 9/18/1954    • DIED: 2/22/2007    • PLAYED FOR TEAM: 1976–77 TO 1979–80

Dennis Johnson was a great defender who worked hard to become a dangerous scorer, too. No player was more important to the Sonics in the late 1970s. DJ was an All-Star twice in Seattle.

## GUS WILLIAMS                                  6´ 2˝ Guard

- BORN: 10/10/1953    • PLAYED FOR TEAM: 1977–78 TO 1983–84

Gus Williams was known as the "Wizard" because he was magical with a basketball in his hands. Williams had a knack for squeezing through small openings near the basket. He was at his best in the playoffs.

## JACK SIKMA                    6´ 11˝ Center

- BORN: 11/14/1955

- PLAYED FOR TEAM: 1977–78 TO 1985–86

Jack Sikma was a tough competitor. He helped the Sonics reach the NBA Finals in each of his first two seasons. Sikma retired with Seattle's career records for rebounds and free throws made.

**RIGHT**: Jack Sikma

## XAVIER McDANIEL                                    6′ 7″ Forward

- BORN: 6/1/1963     • PLAYED FOR TEAM: 1985–86 TO 1990–91

Xavier McDaniel was a handful for any opponent. He had the skills of a small forward in the body of a power forward. The "X-Man" combined with Dale Ellis and Tom Chambers to give Seattle a terrifying scoring trio in the 1980s.

## NATE McMILLAN                                       6′ 5″ Guard

- BORN: 8/3/1964     • PLAYED FOR TEAM: 1986–87 TO 1997–98

Nate McMillan played every game of his NBA career with the Sonics. He was a smart and *versatile* guard who was also a tough defender. After his playing career, he returned to Seattle and coached the Sonics for five seasons.

**SEATTLE**

GARY PAYTON
SUPERSONICS' GUARD

## GARY PAYTON                                         6′ 4″ Guard

- BORN: 7/23/1968
- PLAYED FOR TEAM: 1990–91 TO 2002–03

Gary Payton was known as the "Glove" because he covered his man so tightly. He was just as talented running Seattle's offense. Payton made the All-Star team nine times and was named Defensive Player of the Year in 1995–96.

## KEVIN DURANT      6′ 9″ Forward

- BORN: 9/29/1988
- FIRST SEASON WITH TEAM: 2007–08

Fans marveled at Kevin Durant's ability to shoot, dribble, and rebound, especially for a player his size. He was the **Rookie of the Year** in 2007–08 and the MVP of the 2012 **All-Star Game**. Durant led the league in points in five of his first seven seasons.

## RUSSELL WESTBROOK     6′ 3″ Guard

- BORN: 11/12/1988
- FIRST SEASON WITH TEAM: 2008–09

Few point guards in history have attacked the basket like Russell Westbrook. He joined the Thunder at age 19 and became an All-Star in his second season. When the playoffs rolled around, Westbrook took his game to an even higher level.

## SERGE IBAKA      6′ 10″ Center

- BORN: 9/18/1989    • FIRST SEASON WITH TEAM: 2009–10

Serge Ibaka was eager to learn the ins and outs of pro basketball when he joined the Thunder. He developed into one of the NBA's best shot-blockers and rebounders. In a 2011–12 game, Ibaka recorded a triple-double with 14 points, 15 rebounds, and 11 blocks.

**LEFT**: Gary Payton    **ABOVE**: Kevin Durant

# Calling the Shots

Thunder fans demand a lot from their coaches, and their coaches demand a lot of the Thunder. This *tradition* stretches all the way back to the 1960s, when the Sonics joined the NBA. Lenny Wilkens started his career as a player in Seattle in 1968 and became the team's player-coach the following season. In 1971–72, he led the Sonics to their first winning record. Seattle fans were thrilled when Wilkens returned to the sidelines in 1977–78. He guided the team to the NBA Finals two years in a row and also to its first championship.

Over the years, the Sonics hired more former players to coach the team. Nate McMillan was known around Seattle as "Mr. Sonic." He led the club in the early years of the 21st *century*. He was followed by Bob Weiss, a member of the original Sonics in 1967–68.

Other coaches who helped mold Seattle into a winner were Bernie Bickerstaff and George Karl. Bickerstaff was very good at working with young players. He rebuilt the Sonics in the 1980s and led them to the Western Conference Finals in 1986–87. Karl got the team to within two victories of a second NBA championship. In each of his seven seasons with the Sonics, they went to the playoffs.

In 2007–08, Scott Brooks joined the team as an assistant to head coach P.J. Carlesimo. The following year, after the team moved to Oklahoma City, Brooks was promoted to head coach. Brooks had been a bench player in the NBA for 10 years and helped the Houston Rockets win a championship. In his first five full seasons as the Thunder's coach, the team won four division titles. He was named the 2010 Coach of the Year.

**LEFT**: Lenny Wilkens talks to his players during a timeout.  **ABOVE**: Scott Brooks shows his Coach of the Year trophy to the Thunder fans.

# One Great Day

At the start of the 2012 Western Conference Finals, experts predicted that the experienced San Antonio Spurs would defeat the up-and-coming Thunder. After the Spurs won the first two games, most fans thought the series was over. But Oklahoma City responded with two victories at home, and then the Thunder won Game 5 in San Antonio. Suddenly, they were one win away from their first conference title.

More than 18,000 fans packed into the team's arena for Game 6. The Spurs came out flying and caught the Thunder by surprise, opening an 18-point lead late in the second quarter. Oklahoma City turned the tables in the second half. The Thunder dug in on defense and raised their energy level. They drew even early in the third quarter.

The exhausted Spurs were left flat-footed. They committed nine fouls in the first seven minutes of the fourth quarter. Meanwhile,

Russell Westbrook leads the cheers after the Thunder's first Western Conference championship.

Derek Fisher and James Harden nailed long **3-pointers** to give the Thunder a six-point lead.

As the final seconds ticked away on Oklahoma City's 107–99 victory, the fans stood and cheered. Kevin Durant, who finished with 34 points and 15 rebounds, knew how far the team had come, and how important the fans were to the team's success. "It felt good for the city, knowing where we came from and how hard we worked," he says.

Russell Westbrook, who chipped in 25 points, was especially proud of how the team came back in the third quarter. "We got into halftime, the guys came together and said we can come out with this win," he remembers. "That's Thunder basketball!"

# Legend Has It

## Which Thunder star was nicknamed after computer equipment?

**LEGEND HAS IT** that Serge Ibaka was. Ibaka's job as Oklahoma City's center was to keep opponents from scoring near the basket. In 2011–12, he was the runner-up as NBA Defensive Player of the Year. Ibaka was so good at swatting shots that some people called him "I-blocka," but he was better known as the "Serge Protector." Surge protectors keep bursts of electricity from destroying computers.

**ABOVE**: Serge Ibaka signed this photo. Another nickname for him might be The Tongue!

# Which Sonic beat the NBA in the U.S. Supreme Court?

**LEGEND HAS IT** that Spencer Haywood did. Haywood became a member of the Sonics when he was 21. Back then, the NBA had a rule that prevented players his age or younger from joining the league. Haywood sued the league to earn the right to play, and the case went to the highest court in the land. The *Supreme Court* decided in Haywood's favor. After that, many more players jumped straight to the NBA before their college class graduated.

# Which Thunder star drove a motor home through a cornfield?

**LEGEND HAS IT** that Russell Westbrook did. Westbrook was famous for wearing glasses with no lenses in them. In a funny commercial for ESPN, he mistakenly swaps those glasses for Jeff Van Gundy's glasses. As Van Gundy wonders why his glasses have no lenses, Westbrook plows a huge RV through a cornfield in the middle of the night because he can't see out of the thick reading glasses he's wearing!

**H**eading into the 1971–72 season, the Sonics and their fans were very optimistic. The team had been in the NBA for just four years, and things were starting to fall in place. Spencer Haywood, Lenny Wilkens, and Dick Snyder gave Seattle three good scorers. Don Smith had a great year at center. The Sonics would go on to record their first winning season.

**SPENCER HAYWOOD**
SUPER SONICS' FORWARD

Late in the year, however, Mother Nature tried to rain on Seattle's parade— *literally*. The Atlanta Hawks came to town for a game on a stormy night. The Sonics were on a roll. They had won 12 of their last 14 games.

In Seattle, which is famous for its wet weather, the first thing a basketball team needs is an arena with a good roof. This was not the case with the Seattle Center Coliseum. During the game against the Hawks, water dripped on the floor faster than the towel boys could mop it up.

The players were careful to avoid the damp spots, but Haywood and Snyder both slipped and fell at different times. Their injuries caused them to miss the remainder of the season. The Sonics beat the Hawks that night, but they had lost something far greater. Seattle dropped eight of its final nine games and missed the playoffs!

The Sonics had to deal with a leaky roof again more than a ***decade*** later. In January of 1986, Seattle was set to host the Phoenix Suns. Once again, the weather was bad, and drops of water fell on the court. This time, the game was called off. Today, players from both teams can say they were part of the NBA's first rainout!

**LEFT**: Spencer Haywood was one of two Sonics injured during the game against the Hawks.  **ABOVE**: The Seattle Center Coliseum

In Seattle, Sonics fans were known for being loud and proud. The people of Oklahoma City know about team spirit, too. Football may be their first love, but basketball has become a close second. After Hurricane Katrina struck New Orleans in 2005, the Hornets were invited to make their home in Oklahoma City for two seasons. The fans filled the arena night after night to show that they were ready to support an NBA team. Thunder fans also cheer for the Thunder Girls dance team. They perform for the crowd during timeouts.

The name "Thunder" makes basketball fans think of the state's famous storms. However, it also honors Oklahoma's Native American *folklore* and traditions. Thunder plays an important role in the history of that culture.

**LEFT**: The Thunder know how to get their fans excited during games.
**ABOVE**: Seattle fans wore this button to coach Bill Russell's first game, in 1973.

The basketball season is played from October through June. That means each season takes place at the end of one year and the beginning of the next. In this timeline, the accomplishments of the Sonics and Thunder are shown by season.

**1973–74**
Fred Brown scores
58 points in a game.

**1986–87**
Tom Chambers is named
MVP of the All-Star Game.

**1967–68**
The Sonics play
their first season.

**1975–76**
Slick Watts leads
the NBA in steals.

**1978–79**
The Sonics win the
NBA championship.

SLICK

Fans wore this
Slick Watts button
in the 1970s.

Basketball

Jack Sikma

Jack Sikma
starred for the
1979 champs.

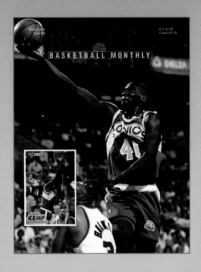

Shawn Kemp was front-page news in 1995–96.

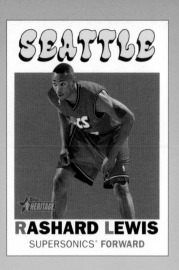

Rashard Lewis

**1995–96**
The Sonics return to the NBA Finals.

**2004–05**
Rashard Lewis is named an All-Star.

**2009–10**
Kevin Durant wins his first NBA scoring crown.

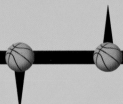  

**1991–92**
Dana Barros leads the NBA in 3-point shooting.

**2008–09**
The team moves to Oklahoma City.

**2011–12**
The Thunder reach the NBA Finals.

Dana Barros launches a 3-pointer.

# Fun Facts

### DISAPPEARING ACT

During the 1977–78 season, center Marvin Webster blocked 162 shots and grabbed 1,035 rebounds. Seattle fans called him the "Human Eraser" because he made so many shots disappear.

### UNLUCKY NUMBERS

In a 1989–90 game against the Milwaukee Bucks, Dale Ellis scored 53 points and set a record by playing 69 minutes. Xavier McDaniel played 68 minutes. The Sonics lost 155–154 in five overtimes!

### THEY'RE HISTORY

When the Thunder began playing in Oklahoma City, they agreed to give up their official "history" if the NBA placed another team in Seattle. This agreement is similar to the deal the Cleveland Browns football team made in 1996 after moving to Baltimore and becoming the Ravens. A new club called the Browns began playing in Cleveland in 1999 and took back the team's 50-year history.

## IN THE BLACK

During the 2012 playoffs, Oklahoma City fans often came to games wearing jet-black beards in honor of James Harden. One office building owner actually hung a giant beard over the entrance to the lobby.

## TRIPLE THREAT

In 2005–06, Ray Allen broke the NBA mark for 3-pointers in a season. He finished the year with 269.

## STAR POWER

In 2012, Kevin Durant starred in the movie *Thunderstruck*. In the story, he loses his basketball skills when they are transferred to a teenager through a magic ball. Acting was easy, Durant says. Pretending he couldn't shoot anymore was the hard part.

**ABOVE**: Thunder fans loved James Harden and his beard.

# Talking Basketball

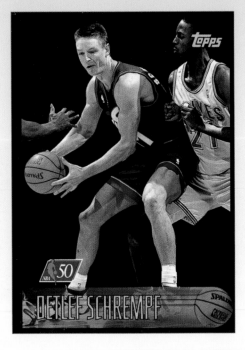

"We knew sometimes going into the game that teams were scared to play us because of the way we were playing."

▶ **Detlef Schrempf,** *on how the Sonics overpowered teams in the 1990s*

"We should have gone in there thinking we could beat them. By the time we figured out we were equal to that team, it was too late."

▶ **Gary Payton,** *on the NBA Finals loss to Michael Jordan and the Chicago Bulls*

"I love our fans. I think we have the best fans in the league. It feels like college again for me, how the fans react to the way we play."

▶ **Russell Westbrook,** *on the enthusiasm of Thunder fans*

"If you want to be a great shooter, you have to shoot the same way every time."
► **Ray Allen,** *on learning to be consistent*

"I'll play all five positions if my team needs me to."
► **Kevin Durant,** *on being a team player*

"Nate is the glue to this team."
► **George Karl,** *on Nate McMillan's value to the Sonics*

"'Russ' does one thing that stands out to me. He gives everybody ***swagger***."
► **Kendrick Perkins,** *on Russell Westbrook*

**LEFT**: Detlef Schrempf     **ABOVE**: Ray Allen

# Great Debates

**P**eople who root for the Sonics and Thunder love to compare their favorite moments, teams, and players. Some debates have been going on for years! How would you settle these classic basketball arguments?

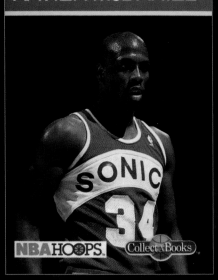

XAVIER McDANIEL

## Xavier McDaniel was the team's all-time best player off the bench ...

... because in 1988–89 he averaged 20.5 points per game as the sixth man. McDaniel (LEFT) was normally a starter, but that season coach Bernie Bickerstaff used Michael Cage, Alton Lister, and Derrick McKey on the front line to begin games. McDaniel would wait until an opponent showed a weakness, and then go in and attack it.

## Wait a second. James Harden deserves that honor ...

... because he actually won the NBA Sixth Man Award. In 2011–12, Harden averaged 16.8 points a game on a team that already had two excellent scorers. In one game, he poured in 40 points off the bench. At 22, Harden was the second-youngest player ever to be named the league's best sixth man.

## Downtown Fred Brown's last basket in the 1979 NBA Finals was the greatest shot in team history ...

... because it broke the spirit of the Washington Bullets—and set up the Sonics' one and only championship. Seattle was ahead in the series, but the Bullets weren't about to give up. Brown came off the bench in Game 5 and hit six of his first nine shots to give his team a slim lead in the fourth quarter. His seventh and final basket of the game was a perfect 24-footer. As Brown released the ball, Elvin Hayes crashed into him and was whistled for a foul. Brown missed the free throw, but the damage was done. Seattle went on to win, 97–93.

## Tremendous shot, but not the best. Serge Ibaka's effort in the 2011 Slam Dunk Contest was the greatest ...

... because no one had ever made (or even tried) his dunk before. A little boy pointed to a stuffed animal attached to the rim and asked Ibaka (RIGHT) to get it down for him. Ibaka soared to the hoop, picked the toy off the rim in his teeth, and then slammed the ball through the basket. Earlier in the contest, Ibaka dunked from the foul line—something only a handful of players have ever done.

# For the Record

The great Sonics and Thunder teams and players have left their marks on the record books. These are the "best of the best" …

Gary Payton

Lenny Wilkens (spelled Wilkins on this card) was the 1971 All-Star Game MVP.

## THUNDER AWARD WINNERS

### ROOKIE OF THE YEAR
| | |
|---|---|
| Kevin Durant | 2007–08 |

### MOST IMPROVED PLAYER
| | |
|---|---|
| Dale Ellis | 1986–87 |

### 3-POINT SHOOTOUT CHAMPION
| | |
|---|---|
| Dale Ellis | 1988–89 |

### SLAM DUNK CHAMPION
| | |
|---|---|
| Desmond Mason | 2000–01 |

### NBA FINALS MVP
| | |
|---|---|
| Dennis Johnson | 1978–79 |

### DEFENSIVE PLAYER OF THE YEAR
| | |
|---|---|
| Gary Payton | 1995–96 |

### ALL-STAR GAME MVP
| | |
|---|---|
| Lenny Wilkens | 1970–71 |
| Tom Chambers | 1986–87 |
| Kevin Durant | 2011–12 |

### COACH OF THE YEAR
| | |
|---|---|
| Scott Brooks | 2009–10 |

### SIXTH MAN AWARD
| | |
|---|---|
| James Harden | 2011–12 |

# THUNDER ACHIEVEMENTS

| ACHIEVEMENT | SEASON |
| --- | --- |
| Western Conference Champions | 1977–78 |
| Pacific Division Champions | 1978–79 |
| Western Conference Champions | 1978–79 |
| NBA Champions | 1978–79 |
| Pacific Division Champions | 1993–94 |
| Pacific Division Champions | 1995–96 |
| Western Conference Champions | 1995–96 |
| Pacific Division Champions | 1996–97 |
| Pacific Division Champions | 1997–98 |
| Northwest Division Champions | 2004–05 |
| Northwest Division Champions | 2010–11 |
| Northwest Division Champions | 2011–12 |
| Western Conference Champions | 2011–12 |
| Northwest Division Champions | 2012–13 |
| Northwest Division Champions | 2013–14 |

Dale Ellis shows perfect form on his jump shot. He was one of the league's most dangerous scorers when he played for the Sonics in the 1990s.

Kevin Durant dunks during the 2009 All-Star weekend. He was voted the game's MVP in 2012.

# Pinpoints

The history of a basketball team is made up of many smaller stories. These stories take place all over the map—not just in the city a team calls "home." Match the pushpins on these maps to the **TEAM FACTS**, and you will begin to see the story of the Sonics and Thunder unfold!

# TEAM FACTS

1 Oklahoma City, Oklahoma—*The Thunder played their first season here in 2008–09.*

2 Seattle, Washington—*The Sonics played here from 1967–68 to 2007–08.*

3 Elkhart, Indiana—*Shawn Kemp was born here.*

4 Penn Hills, Pennsylvania—*George Karl was born here.*

5 Brooklyn, New York—*Lenny Wilkens was born here.*

6 Oakland, California—*Gary Payton was born here.*

7 Pineville, Louisiana—*Rashard Lewis was born here.*

8 Silver City, Mississippi—*Spencer Haywood was born here.*

9 Milwaukee, Wisconsin—*Fred Brown was born here.*

10 Merced, California—*Ray Allen was born here.*

11 Brazzaville, Republic of the Congo—*Serge Ibaka was born here.*

12 Leverkusen, Germany—*Detlef Schrempf was born here.*

Ray Allen

# Glossary

**Basketball Words**
**Vocabulary Words**

**3-POINTERS**—Baskets made from behind the 3-point line.

**ALL-STAR**—A player selected to play in the annual All-Star Game.

**ALL-STAR GAME**—The annual game in which the best players from the East and the West play against each other.

**ALLEY-OOP**—A pass thrown to a teammate as he begins to jump that enables him to dunk before he comes down.

**AMERICAN BASKETBALL ASSOCIATION (ABA)**—The basketball league that played for nine seasons starting in 1967.

**ASSISTS**—Passes that lead to baskets.

*CENTURY*—A period of 100 years.

**CONTENDER**—A team that competes for a championship.

*DECADE*—A period of 10 years; also specific periods, such as the 1950s.

**DRAFT**—The annual meeting during which NBA teams choose from a group of the best college and foreign players.

*ERA*—A period of time in history.

*FOLKLORE*—Customs, tales, sayings, dances, or art forms preserved among a group of people.

**FREE AGENT**—A player who is allowed to sign with any team that wants him.

**HALL OF FAMER**—A player voted into the Hall of Fame, the museum in Springfield, Massachusetts where the game's greatest players are honored.

*LOGO*—A symbol or design that represents a company or team.

*MERGE*—Join forces.

**MOST VALUABLE PLAYER (MVP)**—The annual award given to the league's best player; also given to the best player in the league finals and All-Star Game.

**NATIONAL BASKETBALL ASSOCIATION (NBA)**—The professional league that has been operating since 1946–47.

**NBA FINALS**—The playoff series that decides the champion of the league.

**OVERTIME**—The extra period played when a game is tied after 48 minutes.

**PACIFIC DIVISION**—A group of teams that play in a region that is close to the Pacific Ocean.

*PACIFIC NORTHWEST*—The coastal regions of Oregon, Washington, and British Columbia, Canada.

**PLAYER-COACH**—A person who plays for a team and coaches it at the same time.

**PLAYOFFS**—The games played after the season to determine the league champion.

**PROFESSIONAL**—A player or team that plays a sport for money.

**ROOKIE OF THE YEAR**—The annual award given to the league's best first-year player.

*SUPREME COURT*—The highest court in the United States.

*SWAGGER*—Confidence.

*TRADITION*—A belief or custom that is handed down from generation to generation.

**TRIPLE-DOUBLE**—A game in which a player records double-figures in three different statistical categories.

*VERSATILE*—Able to do many things well.

**VETERANS**—Players with great experience.

**WESTERN CONFERENCE**—A group of teams that play in the West. The winner of the Western Conference meets the winner of the Eastern Conference in the league finals.

**WESTERN CONFERENCE FINALS**—The playoff series that determines which team from the West will play the best team in the East for the NBA championship.

# FAST BREAK

**TEAM SPIRIT** introduces a great way to stay up to date with your team! Visit our **FAST BREAK** link and get connected to the latest and greatest updates. **FAST BREAK** serves as a young reader's ticket to an exclusive web page—with more stories, fun facts, team records, and photos of the Sonics and Thunder. Content is updated during and after each season. The **FAST BREAK** feature also enables readers to send comments and letters to the author! Log onto:

**www.norwoodhousepress.com/library.aspx**

and click on the tab: **TEAM SPIRIT** to access **FAST BREAK**.

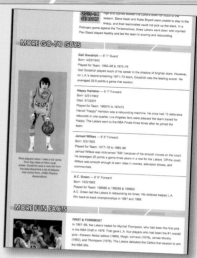

Read all the books in the series to learn more about professional sports. For a complete listing of the baseball, basketball, football, and hockey teams in the **TEAM SPIRIT** series, visit our website at:

**www.norwoodhousepress.com/library.aspx**

## On the Road

**OKLAHOMA CITY THUNDER**
100 West Reno Avenue
Oklahoma City, Oklahoma 73102
(405) 208-4800
www.nba.com/thunder

**NAISMITH MEMORIAL
BASKETBALL HALL OF FAME**
1000 West Columbus Avenue
Springfield, Massachusetts 01105
(877) 4HOOPLA
www.hoophall.com

## On the Bookshelf

To learn more about the sport of basketball, look for these books at your library or bookstore:

• Doeden, Matt. *Basketball Legends In the Making*. North Mankato, Minnesota: Capstone Press, 2014.

• Rappaport, Ken. *Basketball's Top 10 Slam Dunkers*. Berkeley Heights, New Jersey: Enslow Publishers, 2013.

• Silverman, Drew. *The NBA Finals*. Minneapolis, Minnesota: ABDO Group, 2013.

# Index

PAGE NUMBERS IN **BOLD** REFER TO ILLUSTRATIONS.

## THE TEAM

**MARK STEWART** has written more than 40 books on basketball, and over 150 sports books for kids. He grew up in New York City during the 1960s rooting for the Knicks and Nets, and was lucky enough to meet many of the stars of those teams. Mark comes from a family of writers. His grandfather was Sunday Editor of *The New York Times* and his mother was Articles Editor of *The Ladies' Home Journal* and *McCall's*. Mark has profiled hundreds of athletes over the last 20 years. He has also written several books about his native New York, and New Jersey, his home today. Mark is a graduate of Duke University, with a degree in History. He lives with his daughters and wife Sarah overlooking Sandy Hook, New Jersey.